I0521515

My Heart
&
Her Pieces

ELYSSA LATHAM

My Heart and and Her Pieces

A Collection of Poetry and Prose

My Heart & Her Pieces
Copyright © 2022 by Minimal Heart Press LLC.

All rights reserved. No part of this publication may be reproduced, distributed, or transmitted in any form by any means, including photocopying, recording, or other electronic methods without the prior written permission of the author, except in the case of brief quotations embodied in reviews and certain other noncommercial uses permitted by copyright law. For permission requests, write to the author at the address below.

1870 The Exchange,
SUITE 200-44
ATLANTA, GA 30339

Cover Design by Katarina Naskovski
Edited by Sarah Newton-John & Eva Xan
Printed in USA 2022
Paperback ISBN: 979-8-9862849-0-3
Ebook ISBN: 979-8-9862849-1-0

This book is dedicated to you, the reader.
Please enjoy what resonates and take care of yourself.

Trigger Warning this book contains topics of suicide,
self harm, and death.

Table of Contents

All That Flows In   1
Must Flow Out   65
About the Author   141

All
That
Flows In

Selfless One

No matter what they say,
I'll always know who I am.
I am the girl with every heavenly body on her back,
the one who waters withering flowers with her tears,
and the girl who loves more than the blood in her body.
I know I am.

Your Cheapest Thrill

We were in love
for what felt like forever,
but I loved you for even longer.
Ever since the day I met you,
my heart crawled into your lap and bled it's love,
but I never knew quite why it did.

It could've been love
or temporary affection,
for your wandering eyes were always set on my body's scarred
complexion.
You used me and bruised me in a million ways.
From the first time we met, I was your ashtray.
Burning me with every touch.

The day you came back into my life
was the second greatest and worst day I ever had.
The greatest day was the one I met you.
On both days, I gained and lost two valuable things:
you and my will.
I loved you,
but were you in love with me?
It seems like I was only a cheap thrill to you…

Pain Imitating Life Lived

When I was around five years old,
you'd set me in the bathtub,
and we'd make bubble beards.
When I gave you trouble about taking a bath,
you'd show me a trick.
Of course, me being young and naïve,
I'd bathe, then beg for the trick you had up your sleeve.
You made it seem like water flowed from your fingertips.
Completely astonished,
I always tried to do it
but never could.

In place of taking those bubble baths,
I'd sit in the tub with the water foaming over me.
The water burned my pale skin into a fiery, red flame.
I learned that if you put your hands up at a certain angle, the
water would hit your face
directly into your eyes.
It reminded me of the windshield of a car—
how the rain splashed against the windshield like tears on a
broken human faced with pain;
It amazed me.

Yet today, I have learned how to do that gimmick,
but only two things were different:
one, you weren't there,

and two, it wasn't water falling from my fingertips,
it was blood.
Soon after,
I was gone too.

Love's Difference

Tears started forming two rivers beneath my eyes,
frequently occurring like your goodbyes.
I loved you
like the sky loves its different hues.
But even the skies change,
just like our passion when it is inflamed.

Fake love and real love are strange.
Fake love runs out,
and real love, I'll never doubt.

But you and I?
We need a goodbye
for good.

She Stole You

I hope you know you have my heart
in your little hands—
all my hopes and dreams
right in the center of your palm.

He helped me through my pain
by teaching me how to love
and giving me someone to love,
and you took that away;
you took *him* away.

I hope you smile at his silly jokes.
I hope you hug him tightly when he's upset.
I hope you do all the things I wish I could.
He didn't break my heart;
he's too pure for that.
You,
the new girl in his life—
you broke my heart.

Rose Boy

He was like a rose:
wonderful,
smelling pleasant,
blushing an exquisite red,
and gentle.
But like all flowers in the garden,
he wilted away.

Golden Heart Locket

I showed my back to you,
and somehow, you shot right through my forcefield.
How am I supposed to forget you
when you won't let me?
It's been over since the first time we went sour,
but you're holding on to me
like I'm your security blanket.

I was the one who cared
unconditionally and constantly.
And your others? The replacements?
They weren't *me*.

I was golden
(and I still am),
but I'm not your gold heart locket anymore.
Let my chain go!

Non-prescribed Medication

It's times like these when I need you—
times when I get
worried,
scared,
and feel hopeless.

And you?
You take it all away
like you're my prescription medication
with no refills
that's recalled every two months due to toxins.
You poison me,
but I am addicted.

Dancing With Choices

I'm stuck
between
easy yet fake love
and untouchable blissful love;
between
being used for love
and exploring what I daydream over.

I'm stuck
between
someone I don't want
and someone I can't have.

Your Ghost is Haunting Me

I can't help but drown myself in our old memories.
Floating past our movie dates and sinking through the music you
played for me.
You are the only thing I've ever known!
Whether it be the harshness of your actions when I spoke about
what haunted my mind
or our good times at home being love drunk teenagers,
you never seem to leave my mind.

It's almost as if you're a ghost haunting me.
Maybe you *are* dead and gone…
at least the person I knew and loved.

Chaos

I live and breathe off the fumes of chaos,
especially *yours*.
The chaos you use to control me
possession seeped from your lips
and poisoned my being.
The pain I cause won't drown it.
"I want to die!" I shout.
There is no good ending for me,
just everlasting torment and agony.

September 18, 2011

Today made me realize
how much of a good person I am.
I remember him
(unlike his mother)
the boy who got neglected,
the boy who was my first heartbreak—
my boy
left for dead by a selfish monster.

How could you let him go to the hospital so much
for neglect if you indeed cared?
Why did you let him get dehydrated?
Why did you mistreat my sunshine like that?
Don't you dare say it was an accident!
That family did not care.
My family would have killed innocents
without hesitation for him.

It's been eleven years,
and I always think the same thing:
Why not me instead?

Vacant Friendship

Don't get me wrong…
We did have memories,
just no connection now.

It took me months to figure out what changed in us.
When you came over to stay the night,
we shared laughs,
we caught up on the drama,
and just did best friend things.
Something in the way your shifting eyes told me you wanted to
bolt out the room
and your nervous hands screamed, "This isn't me anymore!"
But in the morning, I realized
a stranger was lying beside me.

Better Off Dead

I feel your gaze like impacting bullets
watching me from afar.
There's no time for me to run away
from your bloodied arms.
"I don't want to hurt you,"
you say while aiming the gun at my head.
Maybe I am better off dead...

Hotel of a Heart

I harmed myself tonight,
not physically but mentally.
I listened to the music you sent me
'Nothing Else Matters' settled in the background of my suffering
and drifted over to your social media pages.
"In a relationship," they all read…
a month after you
tried to get with me again.
I cried.

At that moment, I realized
you never really loved me—
you just can't stand being alone.
You need a month or two of vacancy
from an innocent girl,
then trick them into caring
and pump false hope
into their veins.

You did not love me;
you just loved the idea of a free stay
at my hotel of a heart.

Change

If the world can change,
hair can change,
faces,
bodies,
everything and anything—
then why can't my heart stop loving you?

Voluntary Suicide

I can find beauty in almost anything:
rain,
grass,
water,
beaches,
but in *him*?
There's nothing beautiful in suicide.

Love or Boredom?

I can't seem to disconnect myself from you.
You moved on,
but I can't seem to take two steps away.

I can ignore you:
Blocked.
And I can go without talking to you all days of the week,
but seeing your chocolate coated eyes makes my heart flutter in
its cage.

Thinking of you cannot be stopped.
Part of me wants you,
and the other knows your intentions.

But the thing is,
I wait for you to message me,
and you never do.
I can't tell if I miss you
or if I'm just bored…

Ages of Love

At age four, I used to think love was smiles and kisses.
At age ten, I thought play-fighting was love.
At age twelve, I began thinking
arguing and sleeping in opposite rooms was love.
At age thirteen, I thought love was the first boy
who showed any interest in me.
At age fourteen, I believed love was letting yourself
get emotionally and verbally mauled
by the one you loved.

I thought every 'I love you' was true,
no matter the person.

At age fifteen, I thought love wasn't for me.
At sixteen, I think love is an indescribable feeling
that is only true when you least expect it.
I still don't know love
and I do not want to
until the right time;
I'm not ready.

Emotion's Vessel

Maybe emotion powers me.
Perhaps it strives to help me.
It's what makes me better,
what keeps me sane.

The depression,
torture,
burning ache
makes me powerless,
but I feel like a god.

Maybe I wasn't in love with you after all—
I was in love with the pain.

Venomous Love

They say having too much pride is poisonous
and it will taint your actions towards others.
I think pride is a lifesaver.
It kept me away from you
all this time;
It kept me happy and sane.

I believe having no heart is venomous;
when people stick their fangs into the heart of their prey
and pump venom into them, making the victim toxic
and keeping them sad and in a state of being irrational towards
themself;
by calling it
love.

Hurting

Unfairly treated,
you ignored me throughout
emotionally beaten,
quiet until I cried out
mentally terrorized,
afraid to go the right route
verbally unidentified,
my voice caved to doubt
physically broken,
though I could not shout
mouth shut.
Unspoken.

Everyone turned against me;
I'm against the wall
about to take a fall.
Don't wait on me—
I'll come around
someday.
Just promise me
it'll stop one day…

Me-to-Me Experience

Today I met a girl at school;
she was small
and wore her hair long and curly,
just like me.

As soon as we made eye contact,
she began to sob.
The teacher told me that
she
gets easily stressed.

Something in me snapped—
She looked tired,
stressed,
sleepy,
hurt,
and like she wanted to die.

Then I wondered,
Does she feel small to the world?
Like a car wreck, it hit me blindly.
I met my anxiety,
depression,
and stressed-out vibe all in one form.
The room is going to explode!

Not Mutual

It was you
who was there before him.

It was you
who laughed at all my jokes.

It was you,
the one person who had the same interests as me.
Laughing at our favorite videos and walking the empty streets of
your neighborhood.

It was you
who begged me to go everywhere with you.

It was you;
the person who mattered.

It was me
that fell for you—
but to you?
It's not me that you need.

Our Minds Suck

When I was 10,
I always wondered why the older kids
never seemed bored.

Now that I'm their age,
I realize why:
Your mind and thoughts
can keep you entertained
but screw you over.

Love All of Me

I want someone who adores me;
someone who smiles rays of sunshine while looking at me;
someone who wants to know
what is going on in my mind;
someone who will listen and be curious about
everything in between the written lines.

I'm not asking for worship,
just someone who will love me
unconditionally
despite my ink-spilled pages.

Loneliness

Loneliness eats me alive,
sometimes making me feel small
and not myself.

Alone is how I do my best work.
Alone with no soul aside from my own;
loneliness sometimes fuels me.

Falling out of Love

I know what falling out of love is.
Falling out of love is late and short responses.
Falling out of love is sleeping in opposite rooms.
Falling out of love is begging your partner
to speak to you.
Falling out of love is no longer knowing who you created a child
with.

Don't tell me I don't know what love is—
I know what it isn't
from experience
and seeing it unfold in front
of my eyes.

Oh Shit

I saw your mischievous face earlier this week.
My loneliness smiled at the ground
and my heart raced for you.

It'll get bad again…

I Don't Want You

My mind drifted towards you.
I noticed your smile,
laugh,
and honey eyes.

I began to miss you, but I didn't want to.
I don't want to smile whenever I see your face.
I don't want to see how good you look in your uniform.
I don't want to think about all the good memories.
I don't want to remember you.
I don't want to feel like this.
I don't want to love you again.

Never Easy

If it was up to me,
I'd be lying alongside you
in your arms and smiling,
but life was never
made to be easy,
was it?

Raging Emotions

My emotions are like raging rivers,
flowing through every part of me
and flooding my mind.

At the center of it all is

                    you

with your deep brown eyes
calling out my name.

I Missed You

I never thought I would feel
the warming and wholesome sensation of you
lying next to me again,
but here we are *now*.

Please don't leave.

In My Horizons

You loved me a little too much;
It harmed me more than I'll ever know.
Your soothing voice was my crutch,
and the way your eyes glowed
put me in a dangerous trance.
That's why I've had enough!

I guess we'll never know
how the rest of our story unfolds…
Maybe we would be better together—
maybe my mind is just under the weather
in hopes of having you
in my horizons again.

Can I Disappear?

The more I think about going MIA,
the more excited I get—
not worrying about checking in with anyone,
not caring,
not asking,
and not "reporting for duty."
Just me, myself, and peace…
something I crave.

Do Me a Favor

Fuck you
for tricking me
into thinking that you cared!

Screw you
for telling me sweet lies
in the place of bedtime stories!

Thank you
for the good times,
but do me a favor?
Fuck off!

My Lullaby

My face is hot.
Your heart is cold.
This fucking hurts.
Please leave me alone!

You Hurt Worse

I want to burn up my lungs.
I want to pollute my veins.
I want to carve my skin.
I want to rip out my heart.
I want all harm possible,
but the pain of you leaving
will always hurt worse.

Who You Are

This game isn't fair.
You can't talk and seem interested
for days at a time
and one day decide you don't care,
then leave me to wonder why.

I don't deserve it!
I thought you were good,
but it was foolish of me
to expect something better.

All they do is leave
when it stops being easy.
You were
destined to walk in,
raise hell in my heart,
and run the fuck out
because that's who you are, right?

Duality of a Troubled Soul

My mind is bright yet corrupted.
My heart is big yet cold.
My hands can hold yet have scars.
My voice is steady yet silent.

My love is real
but not shown.

I have good qualities,
I never judge a book by their cover,
I fully love the special people in my life, and
I remain peaceful despite all the trauma
but they are
overthrown.

Two Souls

I need to do more inner work than I thought…

I have become two separate souls:
one pure and full of love,
another toxic and full of hatred.

Both live with me,
fighting to see the light of day.
How on Earth can I be
these two people at once?

Sleeping Alone

You don't realize you're sleeping alone
until you fall asleep in the arms of the one you love
and attempt to forget the warmth of their body
against your own
when they are gone

That is sleeping alone.

Her Hell

My brain doesn't run free anymore.
She sits alone in a cage
and swirls her finger in hellfire

She's been screaming for my help
for what seems to be decades.

I am so sorry.

Hands

Hands are something special.
They hold life,
craft wonderful masterpieces,
make
and break
your heart in two.

The Creative Craves Sin

I want to bleed out poetry from my veins.
I want to scream out stories from my lungs.
I want to cry sonnets from my eyes.
But I just don't work that way;
I am so broken like records under cinder blocks that scrape away
the music from its foundation.
I desire to host the creative and have its words ride my skin into
existence for art will exist in and out of me.

Who Am I?

The person I used to be was
the sun,
the moon,
the sky,
the oxygen we breathe,
and all the other beautiful
functioning parts of nature.

But now she is gone,
and I don't know who I am anymore.

Heart Functions

The heart works in mysterious ways.
It'll light up and leap for the love of your life,
but as soon as a tear falls from their eyes it swells in pain.

It's Not Me

It's not me,
the girl you see.
I am in camouflage,
away from my self-sabotage.

It's not me,
the one you see.
I'm hiding away,
praying for another day.

War Inside Me

My mind works against me when I'm happy.
It picks fights with me when I'm sad.
It throws gasoline on me and ignites the flame
when I am angry.
It pushes me in a corner and blinds me with negativity.

My mind is my worst enemy,
and our ongoing war will not end cleanly.

4 am Thoughts

It's 4 am, and the only thing on my mind is you,
with that look on your face—
the look of entertainment,
excitement,
achievement…
Is that what I am to you?
A fucking trophy glass
to hold your liquor?

Once this glass of mine breaks,
I might put it in your neck.
Who the hell are you to hurt me?
To take advantage of me the way you did?
I was the wrong one to screw over.

No Angel

You call me an angel
based off my looks
and smile.

I'm no angel.
I am a troubled soul,
drowning in sin,
full of rock-salt tears,
and scars from being stripped clean of my wings.

What angel looks this way?

Nervous

I'm not lazy!
I'm just worried that this will backfire on me.
I'm sorry I can't speak to you.
Your presence makes me so excited
that I am afraid I'll actually
vomit on you and you'll never
speak to me again.

I'm not lazy,
just nervous—
so damn nervous.

Wake Up

When you are alone,
you can become less than yourself,
you can become a foreigner,
someone unfamiliar.

Like nights at 2 am when you cannot sleep,
your thoughts won't
leave you be.
They become violent
and you are vulnerable.

Late at night,
you lose yourself
and gain a monster.
Sleep won't save you,
but waking up will.

Tragic Moments

Use your tragic moments and create
sad ballads out of them.
Put so much
heart,
soul,
and pain into them
that the world understands
what you went through
and cries with you.

The Girl Is Gone

The girl felt her mental stability come undone,
steaming poison in her veins,
contaminating her heart,
breaking her calm voice of reason,
and chewing and spitting out promises.

She wasn't sure from where all this came—
maybe from her toxic mind?
Maybe her soul gave in to its surroundings,
rejecting itself into a labyrinth of filth.

The girl felt her rationality unravel before her,
and it killed her.

Open Your Eyes

You say it is overreacting,
but maybe it's my brain over-compacting
my thoughts into a fact,
based on your little acts.

You aren't safe
and I can't escape.

You there!
Open your eyes
and surprise their little lies.

Your Last Option

I'm the second thing you ask for
after not getting the first.
I'm the runt of the litter.
I'm the child that no one wants on their team.
I'm the dog at the pound that people walk past.
I am your last resort.
I am your last decision,
because deep down
you know,
I am a mistake.
I am the old bench no one uses.
I am the fruit that does not get taken off the tree.
I am the feeling that surfaces after you realize
you raised your hopes too high.
I am worse than difficulty.
I am replaceable.

You Are a Stranger

I can't take it anymore!
Not only do you leave my heart sore,
but you leave me torn—
straight through the core.

I'm incredible to you,
but you beat me blue.

I can no longer grow.
It is you
I no longer know.

My Being is a Mess

I am a happy person who has many bad days.
I blame it on my sensitivity,
my heart,
my fears,
my anxiety,
my depression,
and,
oh yeah!
The chemical imbalance inside my brain.

Sometimes I cry over things that are not true:
false theories I create
and scenarios that will never happen.
My emotions bounce all over the place,
especially if I remember things
that ruin me and my whole day
and notice the one I care about being mistreated.

Sometimes I get angry over imperfections,
not knowing what to say,
being awkward,
not hearing what a person says the first time,
knowing that I am not flawless,
my stuttering,
and just not being my best.

My mind is harmful,
and with its partner in crime:
anxiety,
it is game over for me.
I am sorry if I don't speak clearly,
or I am nervous.
I'm trying my best not to create a bad day
with mistakes upon which
I will judge myself forever.

Happiness and I Broke Up

I haven't been happy for the longest time.
She and I parted ways a long time ago.
Happiness is on vacation,
and she decided to stay gone
because I am too dark for her.

She abandoned me when
the first wall began to crack.
She robbed me of moments when
I should have been smiling,
but I wasn't.

She stole my laugh,
so all I have now is a simple nod.

I live in a world where happiness cannot exist
because if I am happy,
something will happen if I get too comfortable.
Do not tell me I am overthinking it,
or that it is "just life."
I know better.
It's karma for letting my guard down.
If being this unhappy is what my purpose is
or even my job,
I want a break.

Must
Flow
Out

Our Tragedy of a Love Story

I couldn't look you in your eyes
and tell you that you were hurting me
'cause you'd yell and flee.
But maybe I'm not scared of you—
maybe I'm just feeling blue.

You treated me so cruel,
like it was the number one rule.

In our tragedy of a love story
that eventually faded into tedium,
it turned so dull that I finally pulled a "you"
and flew.

Because of You

I didn't want to stop talking to you;
I needed to.
I had to end it
because you weren't good for my health.

You would hurt me like it was your purpose on Earth,
and I can't endure it anymore.

Just remember that
it's because of you.

I'll forever love you,
but please leave me be.

Our Routine

You apologize,
I accept.

You lie,
I cry.

I live without you,
and you die.

Love is Not a Person

People always ask:
"Who's your new lover?"
I remain silent, then say:
"I don't have one."

Now I do—
It has stared me in the face since the eighth grade.
Writing is my true love,
my passion.

It accepts me,
and it allows me to love myself.

Thank You

Of course I care!
Isn't that the trait of a good person?

It's not that I don't love you—
I do—but it's more like the
"thank you for ripping my heart out
because it gave me the inspiration to begin writing"
kind of love.

You led me to discover my true talent:
making my pain into something useful instead of draining
emotional baggage.
And for this,
I thank you.

Future Love

Where are you, my future love?
I want to do a little time traveling,
so lie in my arms
and rest your eyes.

I promise I'll never say goodbye.
Rest your head on my chest
and don't worry about the rest.

You Were an Addiction

Breathe me in.
Cough me up.
Spit me out.
Am I not good enough?
Do I poison you as you poison me?

I breathe you in,
hold you in my lungs;
I don't release.
Instead, I keep holding
until I pass out.

Eventually, you will kill me,
but that was the past.
Now I avoid your drug.

Born Without You so I'll Live Without You

I held you so close:
in my heart,
in my body,
in my soul,
and everywhere you could fit.

I needed you,
I loved you,
but then I realized:
I don't need you.
I'm the one who stitches myself up.
I'm the one who mends my broken heart.
I'm the one who takes care of myself,
not you.

I was born without you,
so I have found
I can live without you.

Your Worst Distraction

I always wondered:
Why did you leave?
I thought it was because I was a distraction,
but that didn't seem quite right.

It finally hit me
like a freight train:
Yes, *I* was the reason you left.
I was a bother to you because
every time you saw me or heard me speak,
you realized how much of a horrible person *you* are.

Every bad thing you did to *me*

cuts *you* up and ruins *your* day.
I'm glad you can feel it too.

Influence

I'll lie in bed and wonder:
"Why am I stuck on you?"
Then I realized: You were my reason for writing.
You hurting me caused me to develop
undying love for this craft.

I realize that
traces of you are found in
everything I write.
Whether about you or not—
you are there.

Repetition

I've written the same thing over and over,
with different phrases like,
'My love for you is stronger than any current in the oceans
around us.'
and different emotions flow through them.
Love floats through all of them while anxiety fights to keep to
the surface and not drown.

There are three words I don't think I'll ever use—
three little words that could change everything:
I forgive you.

The Moon Feels Too

It's the moonlight that makes me feel at home;
the moon staring down at me,
speaking in a loving tone:
"You'll be alright."

The moon and I share things in common:
We shine in the darkness
and it also consumes us,
but the ones we love
leave us for other beings.

Pencil and Paper

We used to go together like
pencil and paper,
but you used all my lead and ripped the page,
leaving me with only my eraser.

I tried gluing your torn pieces back together,
but it wasn't the you I once loved.
I decided to try something new,
to get you out of mind.

I used what remained of you and I.
I obliterated you;
Everything within
or between the lines was gone.

While I cleared you off the page, I gained back my lead,
little by little.
But after you were all gone,
I recognized something:
You were not the paper.
You were only the words my pencil wrote.
So, I begin to write something new:
My life without you.

Time Stands Still

Fantasizing about freezing time was my thing.
Whether it was to get away
or remain in a good moment,
I wanted to stop time from ticking.

As the years of my obsession lived on,
I began to form scenarios on freezing time:
moving stuff around,
messing with people,
observing people,
things,
and ideas without being judged.

Two years later, I learned something:
Time does stand still,
but only when I'm forming beautiful words
that bleed into a new story.
Every person or object may not stop,
but the only thing that makes them seem frozen
is my mind when
I focus on what I love:
writing.

Good at Goodbye

During the times we were together,
I developed different traits.
During our first break-up, I developed paranoia.
I searched continuously for the signs you'd leave me again.
When we got back together, I lost my sense of pride.
I felt weak allowing you back into the heart you once wrecked.
Being aware of not needing you
or the pain you caused
and still choosing to allow you back
was something I learned because
I thought it was love.

But the important thing I picked up on was,
whenever you would leave me
the many times you did,
I became very skilled at goodbyes.

It Will Be Okay

I saw you,
yet I ignored you.
I guess that is a sign I'm moving on...
Resistance to not wanting you is growing!
The memory of the sound of your voice has died.
I'm getting stronger and wiser about my actions,
when I used to consult you,
and that's okay.

Kindness Doesn't Exist Towards Myself

Don't you dare call me a horrible person—
You have no right to!
Bad people don't promise people the world.
It's not like bad people to put their wants and needs aside to
supply them for the wrong people.

I am horrid
towards myself;
I don't give myself enough love or credit
for how much good I actually do.

Books Are Better Than People

Books are beautiful.
They're written heavenly
and designed gorgeously.

Books also have a 'welcome home' smell,
so sweet and cozy.
They don't have hair,
have eyes,
or speak lies in tangled goodbyes.

Books aren't alive,
but they still treat me better
than any living person could.
Books are better than people.

No Good

The good thing about being run by pride is
not sinking and messaging your ex
because you're bored and lonely.

I let that thought eat me alive because
I can deal with myself in the correct way—
Allowing the emotions to flood over before I drown.
I can't deal with your lies and mistreatment correctly.
You're no good for me.

I Deserve Self Love

You know what?
I'm tired of being sad and angry all the time.
I want to move on to happiness and self-love
because this down-in-the-dumps shit is getting old.

I want to be my sunshine,
my lover,
my friend,
my caretaker,
and—goddamn it—I will do it!
But I have to self-medicate
and fix this before it
becomes another unhappy era.

I don't have time to be sad.
I need to experience and live.
I need a change.

Where?

Where did you realize that he lied?
Where did you see the truth?
Where did you cry?
Where did you hold your pieces together?
When did you find out that you deserve better?
What did you do for yourself when you realized relationships
aren't what you need to focus on anymore?
Did you finally feel happiness when you let go?
Did your heart beat to the sound of your own drum?

Being out of a toxic relationship is better
than staying in it.
If you're in there,
get out!
I promise, from experience,
it will get better.
Focus on yourself.
Time is ticking!

Exquisite Phenomenon

The world turns,
the sunset glows,
the water flows,
the air fills,
and the grass grows.

All these natural phenomena continue,
and here I am with you,
my exquisite phenomenon.

Moving On

Today was the first day I saw you.
My heart didn't pump to explode.
I didn't even smile.
For the first time in the three years
that I've known you
and used to love you,
I didn't feel a thing
when I saw you—
You're just a face in the crowd,
and I'm actually moving on.

You Are Poetry

I want to write love songs for you.
I want to tug on your heartstrings
instead of your clothes.
I want to show you how much you mean to me
without giving a special gift.
I want to show you your beauty
without speaking compliments.
I want you to be the source of my poetry.

I want you to know,
darling,
you are poetry.

Lover by Compassion's Curse

My heart latches on to anyone.
If you care for me,
seem to enjoy my presence,
or even smile at something I say,
I automatically lock you up in my heart.
That's the scary thing about it.
I'll lock in on anyone nice—
even if,
they spit venom more than sugar
down my throat.

I'm a lover,
not a fighter.

No Longer Your Tribute

Everything I did
used to be just for you.
Every step,
every smile,
giggle,
any word that came from my mouth
was just for you.
My whole existence felt like
a tribute to you.

Nowadays,
everything I do
is to show you
that I'm strong,
that I'm capable of being alone.
My life doesn't revolve around you.
I OWN MYSELF!
And my choices.
Leaving was the best decision
concerning my well-being
I ever made.

I'm not who you remember.

You Are Worth It

When it comes down to it,
you'll always matter to me
more than I do to myself.

You've helped me from the start,
supported me,
and stood by me.

I don't know who I would be
without your advice.
I'd give you the galaxy
and everything that surrounds it—all because you deserve it.

Deceiving Eyes

Eyes like yours
shouldn't belong to you.
Your beautiful brown orbs are
staring down at me
like I'm on a platter
being served to you.

Your darken sinful eyes are
eyeing me down
like I'm your prey,
and it makes me want to
carve them out of your head,
but they are your only good feature.

Manifesting the Good Life

The cards I got handed somehow contained luck—
It was sprinkled all over them.
They glisten with happiness
and shine with positivity.

With all the bad that was force-fed into me,
I deserve all the great things coming my way.

My Devil

Is it sinful that I want to hold your hand?
I want to rub the stress out
of your ash-burned fingers.
I want to kiss the fire-colored skin
between your knuckles.
I want to hold the burning body
that keeps me warm.
I want to look into your fire-blazing eyes
and tell you to come back.
I wish to run my fingers through your flaming hair,
even if my skin melts off.
I want to kiss your lips and taste the flavor of hell.
Because you,
my love,
are my devil.

She Survived

I can't help but remember all the good you did.
Making me laugh whenever my mental health got the best of
me.
I can't help but adore the nice things you did.
Calling me beautiful the small amount of times you did.
I can't help but cry over how hurt I became.
You abandoned me when it became difficult to love me.
I can't help but wonder how you are doing—
if your life got better.
I can't help but think about you texting me
after all these months of silence.

What would you even say?
What excuse would you use?

I can't help but feel guilt for allowing you to abuse me.
I can't help but feel foolish for falling for you
so many times.
I can't help but play the songs you used to send me.
'All or Nothing' sent me into a fever dream of what we could've
been.
I can't help but smile
because all of it went away.
I can't help but be happy
because I lived another day
without you.

3 am's Affection

It's 3 am,
and I'm lying in bed
just smiling my beautiful face off.
I can't help but think
about how far I've come,
about how far I'll go.

I can't believe I'm still here,
even after everything that has
attempted to knock me down—
I am still here and breathing.

Winner

Here I am talking to you,
smiling like I won the lottery
because I met someone that reminds me
that I'm a winning scratch-off ticket.
I'm your million-dollar baby!

Adoring You

Looking at your beautiful features makes me wonder:
Was it all your parents' doing
or did God himself personally intervene?
Did he spill the good looks mixture along
with the positively infectious personality mixture
into the bowels of creation?
You are an absolute goddess.

Love Makes Me Sick

Give me reasons to write appalling love poems
about how you make me feel like I can fly into the stars that
replicate the twinkle in your eyes—
so I can look back and cringe
at how hopelessly in love I was.

Give me emotions I never felt before, so I can
for once in my loud life, be speechless about your love for my
existence.

Tell me all the lies you will tell,
so I can maybe do the right thing and never let you back
into this damaged heart of mine.

Give me my time back, time I wasted on you,
so I can invest it in someone else.
You're a lost cause!
Give me myself back.

My Girl

You make me smile—
a full-on ear-to-ear smile,
especially when I see or think
of your smiling face.

I like the idea of us being a thing:
long walks on the beach,
trips to all your favorite restaurants for dates,
lying around in bed all day
reading or watching Netflix,
you not minding my occasional mindless cuddles,
and me not minding your clinginess.

Deep down, my body is aware of my feelings
and fond of the very idea of you,
returning to my bed a couple more times.
I believe that's why I find myself sleeping on the left because
subconsciously, I want you
on my right side.

Maybe one morning,
I'll wake up to you tangled up to me.
I am falling in love with you:
my girl.

Self Love is the Best Love

If I could rewrite myself,
I simply wouldn't.
There's no need.
I love the young woman I am today.
I am falling for the woman I will be.
I am not conceited.

I just love myself.

Fire's Desire

If it's fire
you desire,
then kiss me,
and I'll light you up
brighter than the night's sky.

Pure Intentions

Never will I ever hurt you.
If I do,
I promise that was not my intention.
My intentions are good and pure,
just like your heart.

The Woman in the Mirror

I never noticed how attractive you were:
pretty pink lips,
hazel eyes,
and a lovely face covered in freckles.
Why did it take so long for me to see my beauty?

Treat Me Right

If it's the rage you want,
provoke it.

If it is my pain you like,
leave me.

If it's love you need,
announce it.

If it's me you want,
kiss me now.

Her Season Changed

The only reason you're back?
You sensed a change.
You knew I had grown stronger
and you wanted to test it.
You saw others seeing me
how you once did;
you didn't like it.
You had to ruin the chance
of me having someone new.
This time,
you won't spoil it for me!

Your End

I know I might not be your first kiss—
Hell, maybe I am…
Either way,
it doesn't matter,
as long as it ends with me being
your last first kiss.
I want to be your endgame.
I want to be your forever love.

My View

The sun throws it's bright beams for you,
the stars twinkle in the sky for you,
the water flows millions of streams for you,
the wild plants that surround us grow for you,
and my heart beats out of my chest for you.

Internal Warfare

My mind is at war with my heart.
It's bloody,
messy,
and it contains no signs of forfeit.

But when I lie in your arms,
I swear the war ends, and the world around me sinks into a calm
slumber.
Please stay.

Never Return Me

I never want to leave your side.
You make me feel so free,
with no worries,
no distractions,
no standards I have to obey—
and my hands are occupied
along with my heart.

You make being myself easy.
You have my heart:
No exchanges or returns.

Stay Here

I like you too much to allow you to walk out of my life.
I enjoy your presence too much to release you.
I don't want to let you go again.
I couldn't bear knowing I couldn't give you
what you deserve.
My heart settled on you and I wanted to be the one to grow and
live beside you.
This time, I might beg you not to go…

There's a forever between us,
whether you see it now or not.
Perhaps in this life
or in another life,
but there's one thing you should know:
I'll be your girl until the end of time.
You might as well stay:
So why don't you?

I Love You Fully

Words cannot describe
how much I love you,
but I can try...
I will only stop loving you
when the sun explodes,
when the stars die,
when the moon disappears,
and when the planets collide.
In other words:
never in this lifetime.

Comfortable in My Skin

I am loungewear material.
I'm best on a lazy Sunday
with nothing to do and no cares.

I am beachwear material.
I shine and glow when the sun
dances on my skin.

I am "going out" material.
Presented the correct way,
I turn heads.

I am whatever I want to be
and wear whatever I want to wear
because I look amazing.

Big Plans

Big things will come my way.
I'll make it out of school alive.
I'll find the happiness I crave deeply.
With all the hell I've been through,
there's not a single doubt.

I'm not cashing out just yet—
It isn't my time.
I've still got a lot of hell to raise.

She's Yours

My heart belongs to a human
with the prettiest amber brown eyes
you've ever seen;
a smile that makes me melt,
a laugh to cure all things corrupted in a world,
arms to bear any inconvenience,
and lips to kiss away the pain.
He is a galaxy
and a hurricane.

He is everything beautiful in nature:
the trees,
the ocean,
the oxygen I breathe.

My Brain is Losing This Time

I'm going to break you down
until you are dust.

I'm going to hold you down
until you give up.

I'm going to fight you
until you learn there is no use.

I am going to make you stop.

Do you hear me, brain?
You will not ruin any more of my good things!

Lesson Learned

Nothing is easy.
If it was,
we would have a detailed instruction manual
gifted to us at birth.

Nothing will last forever.
If so, we would be immortal.

Moral of the story:
Treat everything and everyone
with care and love because
you never know what the future

has in store for you.

Inspiration

Sometimes, I wonder:
How many stories and poems about love
can I write before I tire?
But every time I look at you,
three-thousand new ones burst into my mind.

Red Poppies of My Heart

Decorate me with so much love
that it seeps through my skin
and ignites my soul.

Feed me so much love that
I grow red poppies from my heart.
Make me grow from your devotion.

Starting Point

If you're seeking love,
observe what makes you smile.
When you smile,
that's your starting point.

Shine

The stars shine bright.
Tomorrow, you will too.
Put yesterday in the past.
Make today shine for you!

Lover's Wave

Run your fingers through my ocean of hair.
Pin up the waves that keep getting in your way.
Pick up my seashell of a heart
and listen.
Do you hear that?
That's my love,
vaster than any tidal wave.

Admire Yourself

Love your body
like you love your lover.
Drown yourself in its glory.
Admire yourself,
for you are
a work of art.

From Your Eyes

Let me live in your pocket.
I want to see the world from your eyes.
How do you see me
behind my perfect disguise?

Would you love me still?
Or am I too much?
Am I unbearable to touch?
Would affection spill?
If I had the power,
would love be ours still?

Better Half of Me

You are the source of my creativity.
I'd write you oceans of poetry
and stories to show you how deep my love is for you.
You can look down on me for it,
but this is me
showing you
my heart.

I'm giving you insight into what I see in you
and how much I love you.
You make me passionate.
You make me all the loving things I want to be.
I'd write you something special every day,
if you wanted me to,
to show you I love you.

My love,
you deserve the sun,
the moon,
all the stars,
and more.
I hope I can give you more than you deserve.

Foolishly in Love

You make me senseless!
You make me want to steal the sun
and bribe it to shine for you.
You make me crave pulling the moon
with my bare hands
and rearrange the stars in the sky
for you.

I'll hold water back for you.
I'll kiss your worries away.
I'll give you the world,
if you let me.

Needing You

You are the highlight of my day
and peace to my night.
You are the stitches that hold me together
and a smile that unravels me into little pieces.
You are the person I want and need
for the rest of my life.

Nature is Jealous

The waves are crashing against the rocks,
the wind is blowing,
the sun is setting,
and the sunset is alive dancing to the wind's song.

The temperature drops,
and somehow, you are
the most incredible sight I see.
Your smile steals the spotlight from the sun and your sweet voice
stops the wind's chorus in a halt.
Nature is insecure with you around.

Keep Listening

I've done bad things.
I'll be the first to admit to them:
I've stolen,
cheated,
lied,
and broken hearts aside from my own.
But something I will never do is leave—
leave this world earlier than I'm supposed to.
I couldn't do that to you.
You are all I have;
What we have is good.

I'm protecting you
from everything harsh in the world around us.
I'm holding you together before you give out.
I'm carrying you away from the high tides
that splash around us.
I'm doing all in my power to keep you safe.

Please,
keep listening.

When I'm Gone

When I'm gone,
I hope you smile when you see
an open book on a coffee table.

I hope the smell of coffee reminds you
of all our early mornings together.

I hope crumpled paper helps you remember
how beautiful my mind was,
how my heart cried into my work.

I hope the sight of a stranded pencil
makes you wonder if I'm there.

I hope you remember the good in me,
not the bad.

I do deserve that much.

Favorite Masterpiece

When it comes to you,
I'd break every piece of expensive art in the gallery
to prove you carry more worth.

I'd rip apart your problems with my teeth
to scare future ones away.

I'd kiss every inch of your body to show you
I love all of you.

I'd wrap myself around you like a blanket
to take you out of harm's way.

You get all the best parts of me.

Eventually

Whatever tragedy happened to you,
forgive it—do not forget,
but move on.
Stop spending time on it!
Those thoughts will only bring you down.
Those thoughts are only bumps in the road.
Those horrible moments are detours
towards your true fate.

Your true path is the main road.
These things happen to prepare you for the world.
Don't think you're not worth it
because you can't get over
a rough patch in your story.

Back up and give more force and power,
and you will get over it eventually.

Love Me Entirely

If I am what you need,
throw yourself at me.

If I am what you crave,
take a bite.

If I am what you seek,
keep me in your pocket.

If I am what you want,
breathe me in.

If I am what keeps you going,
hold me tight.

If I am who you care about,
love me entirely.

You Are Worth It

You have to realize
that you will get better.

Slowly but surely,
you will return to Earth
from space's consumption.
You will communicate more,
maybe too much, but they will still
appreciate your voice
because it is better than no voice
and no presence at all.

You and I

For as long as I've known you,
you were always the highlight of my day—
whether it was seeing you
or simply hearing your soothing voice.
Seeing your glowing face gave me hope
that I had a positive future.

No matter how far we stray from each other,
we always meet back in the middle
and resume where we left off.

You have my heart.
You've always had it.

I'm aware that no soul is flawless,
but by the way my heart melts in your hands
and how you hold me against you ever so tightly,
we are written in the pages to be absolutely
perfect for each other.

Pause

Moments of pause are so calming—
moments where you hit a pause in your life
and everything goes on mute,
to view every detail surrounding you.

Close your eyes.
Listen to the loudest thought in your head.
Accept it or change it,
take a deep breath
and hold on to calmness—
and if it isn't there,
reach for it.

Let your mind wander.
Remember: wandering
is helpful, not harmful.

Breathe in
and breathe out.
Open your eyes
and live.

My Heart and Her Pieces

Here it is:
this part of me
no one except you can see,
tucked safely in your hands
away from all evil.

It's now up to you
to figure out what to do
with this information.
Hold this so close
that it becomes a part of you,
heals you fully
and helps you.

This part of me will be your friend.
It will be there for you.
Please be gentle.
Take care of my heart and her pieces.

About the Author

Elyssa Latham (she/her) is a young woman of words, (you have just read 9,000 of them), and she is also an avid reader. Currently located in Georgia, she expresses her love of writing in sharing universal human experiences. You would agree that she is a love poet above all else.

Elyssa's works express strong emotions that many people go through, aimed to get the reader to feel those emotions alongside her. She wants readers to take away the idea that it is okay to allow yourself to *feel* deeply and that you can craft art out of pain.

One of her proud achievements so far in her two decades alive is winning the National PTA Reflections contest twice (in the 9th and 11th grade) with her entries, "Hero Within" and "What Is My Story?". The Ritz Theatre in Downtown Brunswick also put "Hero Within" on display!

What Is My Story?

Everyone always asks me to tell them a story. I stay silent, not knowing what *story* they mean: the stories I write or the story I live. My story isn't like the average teenager's; mine is unbelievable. I fly around chasing and killing evil. Yes, you guessed it: I'm a superhero. You're laughing right now, aren't you? Don't believe me – just ask the people I've saved. They will smile and tell you I'm their savior, and they're glad I'm alive. Trust me, I know they will; these people happen to be very close to me. You're probably sitting there with this paper in hand, asking about how much sanity I have left, or at least something close to it, am I right? Of course I'm right! I'm a superhero and I just happen to be in your mind, controlling you, making you read the rest of this.

I'm kidding; I'm not that controlling (big word there: that). Anyway, back to my story: I make and keep people happy, plain and simple. But if you are wondering what my power is, it's laughter. I can make anyone laugh. I can give a person a random look, and in the next second, they'll be on the ground crying because of how hard they're laughing. (Sorry about your breathing issue. It's not my fault I'm funny and have no filter.) See how I managed to get you to believe that I was a superhero? I mean, I am. Look at my comics... But not that type of hero. I heal others that are broken, and who do I end up saving?

Myself. I save myself.

Hero Within

I am my own hero.
It may sound cliché,
but it's the honest truth.

I pick myself up when I fall down,
mend my own heart when it breaks,
soothe my own mind when I break down,
and hold my own hand through the dark tunnels.

In my story,
I survive.

www.ingramcontent.com/pod-product-compliance
Lightning Source LLC
Chambersburg PA
CBHW030306130626
46549CB00002B/717